W9-BMT-610

7/18

Yosemite National Park

by Audra Wallace

Content Consultant

Nanci R. Vargus, Ed.D.
Professor Emeritus, University of Indianapolis

Reading Consultant

Jeanne M. Clidas, Ph.D.
Reading Specialist

Children's Press®
An Imprint of Scholastic Inc.

Library of Congress Cataloging-in-Publication Data
Names: Wallace, Audra, author.
Title: Yosemite National Park/by Audra Wallace.
Description: New York, NY: Children's Press, an imprint of Scholastic Inc., 2018. |
Series: Rookie national parks | Includes bibliographical references and index.
Identifiers: LCCN 2016051667 | ISBN 9780531233344 (library binding: alkaline
paper) | ISBN 9780531239063 (paperback: alkaline paper)
Subjects: LCSH: Yosemite National Park (Calif.)—Juvenile literature.
Classification: LCC F868.Y6 W335 2018 | DDC 979.4/47—dc23
LC record available at https://lccn.loc.gov/2016051667

Produced by Spooky Cheetah Press
Design: Judith Christ-Lafond/Joan Michael

Published in 2018 by Children's Press, an imprint of Scholastic Inc., 557 Broadway,
New York, NY 10012.

Printed in China 62

SCHOLASTIC, CHILDREN'S PRESS, ROOKIE NATIONAL PARKS™, and associated
logos are trademarks and/or registered trademarks of Scholastic Inc.

1 2 3 4 5 6 7 8 9 10 R 27 26 25 24 23 22 21 20 19 18

Photographs ©: cover: Paul B. Moore/Shutterstock; back cover: Bakstad/
iStockphoto; 1-2: PC Rex/Shutterstock; 3: Russ Bishop/age fotostock; 4-5: Jeffrey
Murray/Getty Images; 6-7 background: Thomas Lazar/NPL/Minden Pictures; 7
center right: Mary Evans/Grenville Collins Postcard Collection/age fotostock; 8
background: Enrique R. Aguirre/age fotostock; 8 bottom left: Jimmy Chin/Getty
Images; 10 background: Tim Fitzharris/Minden Pictures; 10 center right: Joel
Sartore/Getty Images; 11: Corey Rich/Getty Images; 12-13: Jeffrey Murray/Getty
Images; 14: Duncan Selby/Alamy Images; 15: christian kober/Alamy Images;
16-17: Nadia M.B. Hughes/Getty Images; 16 bottom left: Jeff Foott/Minden
Pictures; 17 top right: UniversalImagesGroup/Getty Images; 18 left: drmakkoy/
iStockphoto; 18 center: kathykonkle/iStockphoto; 18 right: NirdalArt/iStockphoto;
19: Robert Bohrer/Shutterstock; 20 top left: Barrett Hedges/Getty Images; 20-21:
Bakstad/iStockphoto; 22 background: stevedunleavy.com/Getty Images; 22
center left: Konrad Wothe/Minden Pictures; 23 background: Donald M. Jones/
Minden Pictures; 23 top right: Danita Delimont/Getty Images; 24-25 background:
George D. Lepp/Getty Images; 25 top: Kevin Steele/Getty Images; 25 bottom:
Rob Hammer/Getty Images; 26-30 background: DavidMSchrader/iStockphoto;
26 top left: Josef Pittner/Shutterstock; 26 top center: tab1962/iStockphoto; 26
top right: withgod/iStockphoto; 26 bottom left: KenCanning/iStockphoto; 26
bottom center: DEA/C.DANI/I.JESKE/Getty Images; 26 bottom right: GlobalP/
iStockphoto; 27 top left: Sumio Harada/Minden Pictures; 27 top right: mauribo/
iStockphoto; 27 bottom left: Sloot/Getty Images; 27 bottom center: DCorn/
iStockphoto; 27 bottom right: Dorling Kindersley/Getty Images; 30 top left:
PhotoProDM/Getty Images; 30 bottom left: Chris Cheadle/Alamy Images; 30 top
right: Matthew Ward/Getty Images; 30 bottom right: De Agostini Picture Library/
Getty Images; 30 bottom left inset: Diana Taliun/Shutterstock; 31 top: elmvilla/
iStockphoto; 31 center bottom: venemama/iStockphoto; 31 bottom: Thomas
Lazar/NPL/Minden Pictures; 31 center top: stevedunleavy.com/Getty Images; 32:
Adam Burton/robertharding/Getty Images.

Maps by Jim McMahon.

Table of Contents

Introduction

I am Ranger Red Fox, your tour guide. Are you ready for an amazing adventure in Yosemite?

Welcome to Yosemite National Park!

Yosemite (yoh-**seh**-mih-tee) is in California. It became a **national park** in 1890. People visit national parks to explore nature.

Yosemite gets its name from the American Indian word *uzumati* (oo-zoo-**mah**-tee). Uzumati means "grizzly bear."

Come along with me to explore the park. I hope you are not afraid of heights!

United States

California

Yosemite National Park

N W E S

This is a view of Yosemite Valley.

Yosemite is famous for its supersized sights. You can climb giant rocks. You can hike to roaring waterfalls. You can even stand next to some of the tallest trees in the world. You will see lots of animals in the park, too.

Overhanging Rock has always been a favorite place for photos in Yosemite.

Half Dome is one of Yosemite's most famous sights.

The last 400 feet (122 meters) is the hardest part of the climb up Half Dome.

Hikers have to hold on to cables to pull themselves to the top.

Chapter 1

Rock Stars

Millions of years ago, rivers and **glaciers** helped form Yosemite. They cut through the mountains there. They left behind a deep **valley**. Huge hunks of rock stand on each side of it.

Half Dome is one of those rocks. It is 4,737 feet (1,444 meters) tall. That is as tall as 47 ten-story buildings. People hike to the top. It is hard work!

El Capitan is another famous rock in Yosemite. Rock climbers say it is the world's toughest rock to climb.

Pacific tree frogs live in the cracks of El Capitan. Can you see one?

Sticky pads on the Pacific tree frog's feet help it hang on to the rocks.

Getting to the top of El Capitan is hard because it has steep sides. The sides are also very smooth. People try to use just their hands and feet. But there is not much to hold on to. They wear safety ropes to stop them if they fall. Yikes! Don't look down!

Climbers find tiny cracks in the rock to hold on to.

II

Yosemite Falls is one of the tallest waterfalls in North America.

Yosemite Falls is 2,425 feet (739 meters) high. That is taller than some of the world's tallest skyscrapers!

Chapter 2

Wild Waterfalls

Waterfalls seem to be everywhere in Yosemite. There are more than 20 of them in the park.

Each winter, snow covers Yosemite's mountaintops. When the weather warms up, the snow melts. The water flows into streams and creeks. Then it rushes over the rocky cliffs.

At certain times, the water flowing down Horsetail Fall looks more like lava!

One of the most famous waterfalls in the park is Horsetail Fall. Each February, crowds gather to watch the sunset there. At the end of that month, the sunlight hits the waterfall in a special way. It gives the water a bright orange glow.

People say the waterfall looks like it is on fire. What do you think?

Chapter 3

Towering Trees

Imagine a tree that is taller than the Statue of Liberty. That is how tall giant sequoias (sih-**kwoy**-uhs) really are! There are many giant sequoias in Yosemite. They are so wide that people once cut tunnels through the trunks of some of them. Then they drove their cars through!

IN THE MARIPOSA BIG TREE GROVE   4595

YOSEMITE NATIONAL PARK, CALIFORNIA

Giant sequoias are among the biggest and oldest trees on Earth.

The best place to see these huge trees is in Mariposa Grove. About 500 sequoias can be found in this part of the park.

The most famous one is called the Grizzly Giant. It is the largest giant sequoia in Yosemite. It is 209 feet (64 meters) tall!

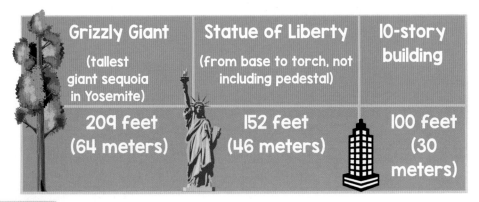

Grizzly Giant	Statue of Liberty	10-story building
(tallest giant sequoia in Yosemite)	(from base to torch, not including pedestal)	
209 feet (64 meters)	152 feet (46 meters)	100 feet (30 meters)

Some giant sequoias are more than 3,000 years old!

GRIZZLY GIANT

Both the great gray owl (left) and the black bear (below) live in Yosemite.

Red foxes like me live in the mountains. But we are hard to spot. What can I say? We are shy!

Chapter 4

Amazing Animals

If you go to Yosemite, be sure to pack your binoculars. You will want them for watching wildlife! Almost 300 types of animals live in the park.

Black bears spend most of their time in Yosemite Valley. They gobble up berries and acorns in the forest. Great gray owls and golden eagles soar overhead.

Herds of mule deer nibble on the green grass in Yosemite's **meadows**. But beware! If deer are around, a mountain lion may be hiding nearby. Mountain lions hunt deer for dinner. Run, deer, run!

A mountain lion can cover 40 feet (12 meters) in one leap!

Tiny pikas and other small animals live in the mountains.

High in the mountains, bighorn sheep trot from rock to rock.

Yosemite is often called a national treasure. More than three million people visit the park each year. They hike Yosemite's many trails and climb the enormous rocks. They fish in the lakes. They raft on the Merced River. Yosemite is full of adventures!

Imagine you could visit Yosemite. What would you do there?

There is so much to see and to do in Yosemite!

These are just some of the incredible animals that make their home in Yosemite.

great gray owl

rainbow trout

golden eagle

bighorn sheep

yellow-bellied marmot

mountain lion

Wildlife by the Numbers
The park is home to about...

150 types of birds   **90** types of mammals

The black bear is the largest mammal in Yosemite!

pika

white-tailed hare

California sister butterfly

mule deer

black bear

35 types of reptiles and amphibians   **6** types of fish

Where Is Ranger Red Fox?

Oh no! Ranger Red Fox has lost his way in the park. But you can help. Use the map and the clues below to find him.

1. Ranger Red Fox fell asleep on Overhanging Rock.

2. Then he woke up and walked north to the park's tallest waterfall.

3. Next, he headed west to climb a big rock. But he was too scared to climb to the top.

4. Finally, he hiked south. He sat down next to the Grizzly Giant to have lunch.

Help! Can you find me?

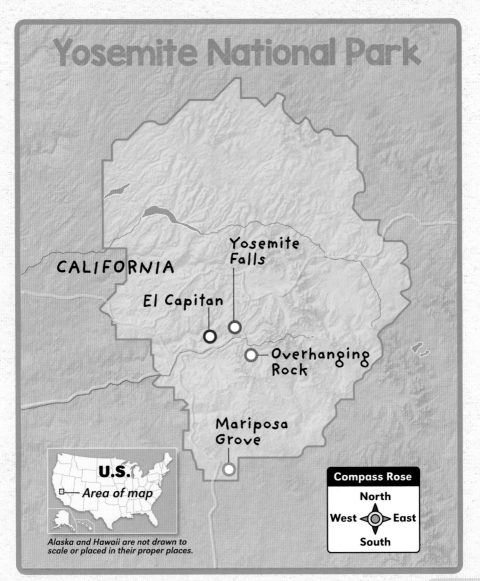

Yosemite National Park

CALIFORNIA

Yosemite
Falls

El Capitan

Overhanging
Rock

Mariposa
Grove

U.S.

□ Area of map

*Alaska and Hawaii are not drawn to
scale or placed in their proper places.*

Compass Rose

North

West ◆ East

South

Leaf Tracker

Can you guess which leaf belongs to which tree in Yosemite? Read the clues to help you.

1. Big-leaf maple tree
Clue: This tree has leaves with five "fingers" and pointy edges.

A.

2. Giant sequoia
Clue: The leaves of this evergreen tree are thin and scaly.

B.

3. Ponderosa pine
Clue: The leaves of this evergreen tree are thin and smooth.

D.

4. California black oak tree
Clue: The easiest way to spot this tree is to look for acorns. Its leaves have seven to nine "fingers" with pointed edges.

C.

Answers: 1. B; 2. C; 3. D; 4. A

Glossary

glaciers (glay-shurz): huge blocks of slow-moving ice

meadows (meh-doze): fields of grass

national park (nash-uh-nuhl pahrk): area where the land and its animals are protected by the U.S. government

valley (val-ee): area of low ground between two hills or mountains, usually containing a river

Index

Facts for Now

Visit this Scholastic Web site for more information
on Yosemite National Park:
www.factsfornow.scholastic.com
Enter the keyword **Yosemite**

About the Author

Audra Wallace is an editor at Scholastic. She lives with her family in New York. She enjoys going on adventures with them, but she is very afraid of heights!